MW00787010

SPIRITUALITY

DRUG ADDICTIONS

RACISM

FINANCE

FAMILY

ALCOHOL ADDICTIONS

EDUCATION

IN THE MIDST
OF THE
STORM

HEALTH

RELENTLESS

JASON JONES

In The Midst Of The Storm

Copyright © 2019 by Jason Jones.

All rights reserved. Printed in the United States of America. No part of this book may be used or reproduced in any manner whatsoever without written permission except in the case of brief quotations em- bodied in critical articles or reviews.

Published by :

Relentless Publishing House, LLC

www.relentlesspublishing.com

ISBN: **978-1-948829-24-3**

First Edition : August 2019

Author photos by Milton Warden

10 9 8 7 6 5 4 3 2 1

Dedication

I would like to dedicate this book to my mother Mrs. Johnnie Jones. Thanks for always being there for me.

January 1

Pat yourself on the back and give God all the praise because you have made it to see another new year! Many people cannot say that.

Things to ponder on

Every time you look down your crown slips a bit. Keep your head up high no matter what you have been through. Respect your journey. It's yours for a reason.

JANUARY 2

God is still in the blessings business. There is
nothing you are facing today, that He cannot handle.
Trust and believe.

Things to ponder on

Allow life to take you places, not keep you places.

JANUARY 3

Don't wait until Sunday to thank God. Thank God every day. God is love.

Things to ponder on

Do not regret growing older. It is a privilege denied to many.

January 4

Speak life over your situation. When praises goes up! Blessings come down.

Things to ponder on

No where in the meaning of LOVE is - Hurt, Manipulation, Abuse, Suffering, Disrespect, Cheating, and Mistreatment.

JANUARY 5

Why be dull when God made you to shine like the sun. Let your light shine.

Things to ponder on

Note to self- Can't worry about what I don't have or haven't done. Do what makes u happy. Be your own movement. Enjoy life.

January 6

God! I thank you for the many things and people you have brought into my life. The good and the bad. Thank you for the new seasons and reasons to PRAISE you.

Things to ponder on

Friendships should happen voice to voice, or in person. Texting, tweeting, Facebooking are great for linking but nothing beats the real thing!

JANUARY 7

We have to learn to trust God when we do not understand what is happening in our lives!

Things to ponder on

The minute you settle for less than you deserve, is when you get less than what u settled for. Don't be afraid to believe that you can have what you want and deserve. Strive for excellence in every aspect of your life!

JANUARY 8

Be encouraged, Be Inspired, Be Renewed and Be Triumphant!!! May GRACE carry you to HEIGHTS unimagined. God bless! Hope that every part of your day is filled with nothing but blessings.

Things to ponder on

Be careful what u ask for! YOU might just get it! Your words, dreams and thoughts have power to create conditions in your life. What you speak about! YOU bring about!

JANUARY 9

As bad as it may seem now, God will NEVER give you more than you can Handle. God can't hand you something new until you are willing to let go of the things that are not good for you.

Things to ponder on

I don't trust words. I trust actions.

JANUARY 10

Today be bigger than the situation you are going through! keep in mind that GOD will fix the situation you are in or use the situation as a tool to fix YOU...Keep the FAITH

Things to ponder on

Presentation is everything. If you give people the right impression, they won't have the wrong impression!

JANUARY 11

Live it, speak it, and believe it.

Things to ponder on

You don't have to show them, they will see.

January 12

Faith and prayer are the vitamins of the soul: man or woman can't live in health without them.

Things to ponder on

I know the truth may hurt but it can also heal.

JANUARY 13

Always keep your head up, because if it's down you won't be able to see the blessings that have been placed in your life.

Things to ponder on

Laughter is always good for the soul.

January 14

Be encouraged today that God can do the impossible. He can supernaturally make all of the dreams He's planted inside of you come to pass. What are you focusing on today? Your situation may seem impossible, but God sees it differently. See your dreams through eyes of faith the way God sees them—fulfilled.

Things to ponder on

Most people love titles but hate work - don't fight for the position if you're unprepared for the job... relationships included!

JANUARY 15

Today -You must leave the problems of the day at the door! When God closes one door. He open a new door full of new possibilities! Count your blessing and not your troubles.

Things to ponder on

When your future is bright, others will try to steal your shine! Don't worry- What God has for you, is for YOU!

January 16

Don't give God your leftovers. Don't give Him the part of your day when you are worn out and can't think straight. Give God the first fruits of your attention. Give Him the best part of your day.

Things to ponder on

Loving the wrong person will make you do, say and act in a manner you didn't know possible causing you more pain than you thought imaginable! Meaning – Be very careful who you choose to love!

JANUARY 17

When you acknowledge God through prayer and worship, your steps are ordered and directed of Him. The Lord gives you wisdom and insight concerning all the affairs of your life. Psalm 37:23 says "The steps of a good man or woman are ordered by the Lord and he delighted in his way." Pray for guidance today. Be blessed!

Things to ponder on

Don't miss out on a BLESSING...Just because it's not PACKAGED the way you expect!

January 18

Dear God today, bring back what I lost, help me find what I been looking for and let a good opportunity seek me out.

Things to ponder on

Unhappy people who don't know their place will try to break your spirit. Trust that God's peace is key to not letting them take you there (anymore)!

January 19

There can be no victories without battles. There can be no peaks without valleys. No roses without thorns. With God strength behind you. His love within you and his arms underneath you. You are more than sufficient for the days ahead of you.

Things to ponder on

Whatever is meant to be in your life. Will always somehow finds it way.

January 20

Gods eye is on the sparrow. I know he watches over me. Through the rain, dark clouds and the storm. I still look for the sunshine. Still holding on. Still feel blessed.

Things to ponder on

In your life's journey remember " a bend in the road is not the end of the road unless you fell to make the turn" Think About It!

January 21

The light of God enlightens every heart that draws close to Him. Where there is chaos, He can bring order. Where there is emptiness, He can bring fullness. Where there is darkness, He can bring light. And no matter how deep the darkness is, it cannot overpower the light!

Things to ponder on

Rock your own style and dance to your own beat!

January 22

God gave you another day to get it right. Don't waste it. Be like a ball - bounce ball. Be like the sun- shine. Be like a diamond - sparkle. Be like God - love.

Things to ponder on

Just because the past taps you on the shoulder doesn't mean you have to look back. Keep it moving.

JANUARY 23

When times were tough you knew who to call. When times get good don't forget their number.

Things to ponder on

If you believe you're the best at what you do, you shouldn't be worried about competition. The competition should be worried about you.

JANUARY 24

Faith is trusting in what you have not seen or experience. Just because it hasn't happened yet, doesn't mean it never will.

Things to ponder on

Just like a shoe, if someone is REALLY meant for you, they will just fit perfectly: no forcing, no struggling, and no pain!

JANUARY 25

We spend our lives looking for a soulmate until we overlook the eternal soulmate- God! New day=more blessings! May your day be filled with nothing but blessings!

Things to ponder on

Today, have the courage to eliminate the negatives in your life so your positives have a chance to speak.

JANUARY 26

We all know that old saying, "Ain't where I could be, ain't where I should be, but thank God I ain't where I used to be." Let's move forward in that spirit today.

Things to ponder on

There are SO many things that money can't buy!

JANUARY 27

Your trials are just shaping you for your blessings!
Don't worry about what u lost. Make room for what u
about to gain.

Things to ponder on

She/he has to have four arms, four legs, four eyes,
two hearts and double the love. There is nothing
single about a single mom/ dad!

January 28

Remember the same God who made a way for you last time, will make a way this time. Trust and believe.

Things to ponder on

The lesson is only the quiz. Going through the storm is the test.

JANUARY 29

Give God your problems and allow Him to give you solutions! Do your BEST and let God do the rest, then just STAND! We are here for HIS glory not our own!

Things to ponder on

Only ride with the people, you walked with.

JANUARY 30

If my people, which are called by my name, shall humble themselves, and pray, and seek my face, and turn from their wicked ways; then will I hear from heaven, and will forgive their sin, and will heal their land. Now mine eyes shall be open, and mine ears attend unto the prayer that is made in this place. - 2 Chronicles 7:14-15.

Things to ponder on

Don't stumble over something that's behind you.

January 31

You cannot be free while you are attached to your worries, freedom comes when you give them in prayer to God! Be the CEO of your happiness, not the janitor of someone else's misery. In God we trust!

Things to ponder on

There's a story behind every person. There's a reason why they're the way they are. Don't judge without knowing.

FEBRUARY 1

A set back is a setup for a comeback. I believe it. I speak it. I receive it.

Things to ponder on

You can't put a price on a piece of mind. It's too priceless. Be free, be inspired, and enjoy your day.

FEBRUARY 2

Dear God, help us to see when You have called us to simply be there for people and when You want us to speak. If we do not speak Truth, we speak confusion. Help us to walk and remain in Truth.

Things to ponder on

The only reason some people can't stand you is because they can't stop you and you have the nerve to succeed without their say so.

FEBRUARY 3

Thank God for what you have. Trust God for what you need.

Things to ponder on

You can seek and ask for all the advice in the world, but there are some things that cannot be taught. It has to be experienced.

FEBRUARY 4

We can't expect God to order our steps when we're out of place.

Things to ponder on

Before telling them what you're looking for - let them show you who they are. Get to know them, not their representative.

FEBRUARY 5

May the sun always shine on your life. May the rainbow be certain to follow each rain. May the hand of a friend always be near u. May God speak life into your spirit. May God fill your heart with gladness to cheer you.

Things to ponder on

People often talk about how love and friends are two different things. In my opinion I believe that love is merely the deepest form of friendship.

FEBRUARY 6

We are like pencils. Our true worth lies within us. We are in God's hands and. He uses us. We are sharpened in life by events and situations. We are also expected to leave a mark.

Things to ponder on

You don't need a piece of paper to say whatever is in your heart. For some, your best will never be good enough, just keep working hard and let that be their problem.

FEBRUARY 7

Faith + Prayers + God's will = Results! God will throw
a few hurdles your way only for you to jump higher
and go harder

Things to ponder on

It's a new day! Do not allow anyone who have never
seen what you have seen, been where you've been or
have never done what you've done, validate who you
are!

FEBRUARY 8

The size of your struggle does not have a thing on the size of God's love. Struggles can come to an end, God's love don't.

Things to ponder on

You don't need anyone's permission to be who you are!

FEBRUARY 9

Speak LIFE over every situation in your life.

Things to ponder on

A person who is bitter with the world and who always feels like a victim can drain your energy! Real talk!

February 10

Prayer can cause doors to opened, addictions to be broken, eyes to be opened, joy to be restored, and strongholds to be destroyed. Trust and believe!

Things to ponder on

Some people never get the picture until they are out of the frame.

FEBRUARY 11

Be thankful for all of the good in your life. Enjoy your day.

Things to ponder on

Consider your personal space as the VIP room. Why! Because not everyone should have access to it.

FEBRUARY 12

Don't ask God for a signal! If you going to keep running through the light!

Things to ponder on

It's always somebody out there going through something that makes you feel like what you call problems aren't really problems at all!

February 13

The bible says in Isaiah 43:2, "When you pass through the waters, i will with be with you and through the rivers, they shall not overflow you!" Before your burden overcomes you, trust God to put His arms underneath you!

Things to ponder on

If YOU want to fly then you have to let go of all the things that are weighing you down!

February 14

There may be times you want to give up and let go of Gods hand but He will never let you go. We all have to keep trusting and believing in Him. He will never fail us when submit to His plans for our lives.

Things to ponder on

R.I.P. to negative thinking. It's no longer welcomed here.

February 15

It's easy to praise God during the good times, but the hard times purify our praise. Put your trust in God for your daily needs especially during these uncertain times.

Things to ponder on

The wounds that cut the deepest are sometimes inflicted by those who are the closest to us!

FEBRUARY 16

Be reminded, "God is able"! In Ephesians 3:20 it states, "Now unto him who is able to do immeasurably more than all we ask or imagine, according to his power that is at work within us." We must look to Him first and quit looking to Him after we have done all we could do.

Things to ponder on

Sometimes life disappointment can also be life best teacher.

FEBRUARY 17

No matter how you feel today, always remember that, no weapons formed against you shall ever prosper. That is another promise God will always keep!

Things to ponder on

I often wondered how different life would be if i knew back then what i know now. Hmm!

FEBRUARY 18

You may have to fight a battle more than once to win. Whatever it may be. We all have to deal with something. God will never give you more than you can handle. He knows how much you can bear. So keep fighting.

Things to ponder on

Be blessed beyond your trials, tribulation, and tests.
Let your light shine!

February 19

God has the best return policy. Bring yourself back and He makes you NEW again!

Things to ponder on

Blessings have your name on it. It is no competition.

February 20

Help empower, inspire and love someone today without any expectations! God is still in the blessing business. There's nothing you are facing today He can't handle. Trust and believe!

Things to ponder on

Don't judge a book by its cover, if you don't even read. You never know what's inside.

February 21

Sit, breathe, be aware, relax, experience, enjoy, and embrace God's blessings. Mental stimulation-Release the past, so you can move forward.

Things to ponder on

So often we settle for less, much less than we deserve. Today is your day to stop settling and expect the best!

February 22

Your relationship with GOD is more important than anything, because you know for sure that it is a relationship that will last forever.

Things to ponder on

The moves you make will be misunderstood by those who are not meant to join you on your journey.

February 23

Your trials are just shaping u for your blessing. Get
ready to be mentally, physically and spiritually fit.
Get in shape be ready for the blessings.

Things to ponder on

May you attract someone who can keep up with you
spiritually.

FEBRUARY 24

Faith will get you through any situation you encounter. Pray and let God be God

Things to ponder on

Everybody loves differently. Just because it's not in a way that you want it to be, doesn't mean they aren't loving you with all that they have.

February 25

I asked God for strength, and God gave me difficulties to make me strong! Keep the faith!

Things to ponder on

When we take things for granted, sometimes those things are taken. Be humble.

FEBRUARY 26

You will not be easily broken when God is standing by your side.

Things to ponder on

If people have a problem with you, always remember....it is THEIR problem.

FEBRUARY 27

Sooner or later, things will be in your favor. Go ahead and claim it!

Things to ponder on

Shh! Don't say a WORD, just listen and let their ACTIONS talk themselves right out of your LIFE!

FEBRUARY 28

God intended for us to win, so let's continue to do so. It's amazing how God works when you stay positive and in faith.

Things to ponder on

Some walks you will have to take alone.

March 1

Dear God, I ask you to continue to order my steps, direct my path, and place in my life what I need and not what I want. Feed my soul and make me whole. Amen!

Things to ponder on

Today, seek peace and pursue it. Keep your head to the sky.

MARCH 2

Today is the day the Lord has made. You can grumble about your health or you can rejoice that you are still alive. You can whine because you have to go to work or you can be happy because you have a job. Today stretches ahead of you, waiting to be shaped. What today will be like, is up to you.

Things to ponder on

Don't be naive. The first time it's a mistake. The second time, it's by choice.

MARCH 3

In James 1:12 it states, "Blessed is the one who perseveres under trial because, having stood the test, that person will receive the crown of life that the Lord has promised to those who love him." Sometimes, you have to cry. Sometimes you have to get angry. You have to pray. When you have done all you can, just stand.

Things to ponder on

Do not ask God to order your steps if you're not ready to move your feet.

MARCH 4

There is beauty in your brokenness! Look back over your shoulder for only a moment, just to glance back at what you've come through! Now say, "God I THANK YOU!"

Things to ponder on

One of the best feelings in the world is realizing that you're perfectly happy without the things you thought you needed!

MARCH 5

Your spiritual walk is like a tea bag, you never know how strong it is until you put it in hot water.

Things to ponder on

Let what you love be what you do.

MARCH 6

Anything you do today, do it with love. Walk in love and be love, because God is love.

Things to ponder on

It can take years to get over your past but one conversation with the wrong person can take you all the way back to the beginning. As a part of growth, you have to grow out of some people. A friend of your weakness is an enemy to your greatness. When you move on in life, learn to pack light, and only take the people and the thoughts that can grow with you. If they can't grow with you, they can't go with you.

MARCH 7

Your weakness could never limit God's power. In fact, in your weakness, God's strength is made perfect. God hears our prayers and heals our problems. Trust him daily.

Things to ponder on

Your words mean nothing if your actions don't line up with them.

March 8

We have to thank God for His grace and mercy on a daily basis. I don't know what it is to be homeless, but I thank God we never have gotten to that point! I have been jobless and know what it is to struggle. When I didn't know how I was going to make it, God made a way! Count your blessing and not your troubles.

Things to ponder on

Your health is the best investment you can make and the greatest asset you can enjoy. Life is God's greatest gift, but life-long good health is an individual responsibility.

MARCH 9

Philippians 1:6 states, "Being confident of this, that HE who began a good work in YOU will carry IT out to completion..." Be confident and do NOT speak defeat. Talk, act, plan, and be ready because IT will happen.

Things to ponder on

If you want to change your life, change your relationships. At some point, we realize that we can't spend major time with minor people.

MARCH 10

I pray that happiness be at your door. May it knock early, stay late and leave the gift of God's peace, love, joy and good health behind.

Things to ponder on

There is nothing like Freedom in your mind and peace with your choices.

MARCH 11

Blessed are those who understand God's in
control. Leave all things in His hands and you will
be fine.

Things to ponder on

Some people are ready for a wedding and not a
marriage.

MARCH 12

The trials in your life are just a test. A test of your faith. Be encourage!

Things to ponder on

If you know the real you then there shouldn't be anything anybody can say about you that can offend you.

MARCH 13

It is a Fixed Fight. You can't lose with God.

Things to ponder on

From every wound, there is a scar that tells a story
about how you survived.

MARCH 14

God! Thank you for bringing me this far. My soul is anchored in the lord.

Things to ponder on

Sometimes, you just got to take your hands off the situation and leave it in much more qualified hands.

MARCH 15

Today, choose to release your cares to the Lord. Let Him fill you with His peace and joy. Receive the rest that He promises and enjoy the fulfillment and blessing He has for you.

Things to ponder on

Never try to prove that you are somebody to a nobody!

MARCH 16

As bad as it may seem now, God will NEVER give you more than you can handle! There's a blessing in every lesson! Keep the faith!

Things to ponder on

Isn't your back hurting from carrying all that baggage? Isn't it time to let it go and unpack? Change is good but it doesn't come cheap. Don't expect to hold on to your baggage yet still expect change. Change has a high cost because there are lessons we all need to learn in order to grow. Remember you have worth. You are valuable. You are blessed.

MARCH 17

You will never get a busy signal on the prayer line to heaven. Prayer changes things.

Things to ponder on

Real love does not come with chaos, confusion and drama.

MARCH 18

When you can't find energy anywhere: remember God is the SOURCE of your strength.

Things to ponder on

A SHIP is designed to take you places. So, if your relationSHIP or friendSHIP isn't going anywhere, then it is best to abandon SHIP!

MARCH 19

Life offer but two choices: Be humble or be humbled!
If your day is off to a bad start, keep in mind,
someone didn't start at all this morning. Let's make
the most of every moment because we never know
which moment might be our last.

Things to ponder on

Before you name drop, make sure the name has
weight.

MARCH 20

Even in our darkest hour. God always make a way to shine some light on your situation.

Things to ponder on

YOU want to know who's amazing, beautiful, and has the sexiest smile ever? (Read the first word)

MARCH 21

When we walk in the light, we won't stumble in the darkness. Choose to be happy. Speak life and continue to follow God!

Things to ponder on

Never put someone else on a higher pedestal than the one who created them!

MARCH 22

If you have been through the storm, had dirt on your name. And manage to still holding on! God knows who and what belongs in your life and what doesn't. Trust and let go!

Things to ponder on

If the effort ain't there, you shouldn't be either.

MARCH 23

Healing is a process. Whether it's a mental or physical wound. It's still takes time. Ask God to continue to heal your mind, body and soul to protect you from whatever is trying to attack you.

Things to ponder on

When you know you, look good and don't wait for someone to validate it. Own it.

MARCH 24

Release fear. Embrace Faith. Claim what is already yours while unloading unnecessary baggage. Make room for your blessings. It's okay. God has you

Things to ponder on

Know your worth. Walk away when it's clear the path together is going in the wrong direction.

MARCH 25

We aren't meant to try and do everything on our own.
God is our guide and help. He gives His Spirit, truth,
and wisdom to show us how to live.

Things to ponder on

Life has a way of humbling you down.

MARCH 26

Sometimes we have to let go. Let God and believe this too shall pass.

Things to ponder on

The quickest way to lose what you got! Is to think you got it like that.

MARCH 27

I don't know, but I will trust and not be afraid. --Isaiah 12:2--If you are in one of those times in your life when you don't know what lies ahead, or you don't know what to do about some deep issues, think about it this way. Have confidence in God to say, "I will trust and not be afraid." We don't know what the future holds, but we know who holds the future.

Things to ponder on

Appreciate what you have right now, because you don't always get a second chance.

MARCH 28

God I trust you, I know what you have in store for me is greater than my wildest imagination. For that...I thank you.

Things to ponder on

Just as we see the winter turn into spring, our lives also have seasons, so if you get a gloomy forecast today remember this too shall pass.

MARCH 29

Love, gratitude, faith, peace, happiness, courage, creativity, health, and balance! Still live for the sunshine!

Things to ponder on

It's good to see someone you care about and know they been dealing with some things! Just smile! That's enough for me. Imagination has no age. Let's us all just Cherish this day.

MARCH 30

Trouble won't last always. When you feel like you down to nothing, God is always up to something! The teacher is always quiet during the test!

Things to ponder on

I come expecting nothing, so anything gained or lost will be a blessing and a lesson in itself.

MARCH 31

When I count my blessings, I count you twice! Don't let no one pluck away the seeds that God has planted. Let the truth take root, and cultivate them with belief.

Things to ponder on

If you want blessings, be one.

APRIL 1

People who don't understand your story will never understand your praise.

Things to ponder on

When you look good, you feel good. Being healthy is the new sexy.

APRIL 2

God is the plug. Know that God is working it ALL out for your good! Don't let a temporary trial win!!!

Things to ponder on

Never apologize for being great at what you do! It's not your job to stoop down to lower levels. It's their job to climb up to yours.

APRIL 3

God, be my eyes when I can't see. I give myself away so that you can used me.

Things to ponder on

Life is about bridges knowing when to build them, when to cross them and when to burn them.

April 4

Worry is the price we pay when we stop having faith in God. No road that you travel will not always be smooth or straight. Keep the faith!

Things to ponder on

There's no fool like an old fool but some of these young fools are showing real promise!

APRIL 5

Be blessed beyond your trials, beyond your tribulations and beyond your tests. Be thankful! Peace, blessings, and joy to all things under the SUN!

Things to ponder on

Walk in confident expectation today, knowing that when you sow a small seed of faith you will reap a mountain-sized harvest.

APRIL 6

While the Devil is busy setting traps, God has already given you your escape routes. Pay attention. Be blessed everyone!

Things to ponder on

Beware of wolves in sheep's clothing. Everything and everyone that is good to you isn't good for you.

APRIL 7

God is moving people out of your way so you don't trip over them in your next level! Great minds have purposes; little minds have wishes. Little minds are subdued by misfortunes; great minds rise above them.

Things to ponder on

Touch a heart! Change a mind! Be a friend someone needs! Spread love! Speak life!

APRIL 8

God, keep me near the cross! Don't let me stray away from it. In thought, faith, word, wisdom, in deed, courage, in life, and service.

Things to ponder on

I water you. You water me. We grow together.

APRIL 9

The bible says, "Those who wait on the lord shall renew their strength". Pray for patience to endure times of trial, to keep anticipating, keep hoping, and keep believing. Pray for patience to be patient.

Things to ponder on

To those out there suffering from jealousy, I pray you get well soon.

APRIL 10

God always has a plan for you, even if you can't see the blueprint. Continue to let your light shine and let no one put it out. Be blessed!

Things to ponder on

Nothing is worth having if you cannot enjoy it! Determine that you are going to enjoy where you are today on your way to where you want to be tomorrow!

APRIL 11

Every bad or good thing happening is ALL meant to give you what you need for life, GROWTH! The bible says if you remain humble, all your blessing will come to you. Don't just count them but look at all of your blessing!

Things to ponder on

If you are going to do anything, do it with love.

APRIL 12

On this solid rock I stand! I always try to give God the glory! I no longer question why things happen the way they do. God is in control of my life and I know that's it's nothing else.

Things to ponder on

Goal for today: Don't allow your emotions to push you out of your position!! Don't allow people that are less of you to get the best of you.

APRIL 13

Let go and let God. When you let God think for you, the decision becomes easy because God led you to the answer. Hope that every part of your day is filled with nothing but blessings.

Things to ponder on

Many people want their lives to be different but are not willing to change their lifestyle. If you don't like what you are getting out of life, take a look at what you are putting into life.

April 14

Here we are, trying to follow God into a better tomorrow but still clinging desperately to the things of our past life. No matter how painful, if we are ever going to move forward, a time will come when we have to leave some things behind. Things that mean much to us. Things that have been a part of our lives for years. Things that seem essential, but actually only hold us back. Live, learn and let go.

Things to ponder on

Don't go broke trying to look rich! Act your wage!

APRIL 15

The lesson is only the quiz. Going through the storm is the test.

Things to ponder on

The older you get, some things that used to matter to you no longer matter.

APRIL 16

My secret is simple. I pray.

Things to ponder on

Shhhh! Don't say a WORD. Just listen and let their ACTIONS talk themselves right out of your LIFE!

APRIL 17

Even in our darkest hour, God always makes a way
to shine some light on our situation.

Things to ponder on

Peace from the broken Pieces! The soul always
knows how to heal itself!

APRIL 18

God continue to be a present in my life, I receive your gift. Invite the right people into my life, decorate my destiny and order my steps!

Things to ponder on

Love is sometimes denied, sometimes lost, sometimes unrecognized, but in the end, always found with no regrets, forever valued and kept treasured.

APRIL 19

The stumbling blocks in your life can easily turn into the stepping stones of tomorrow. If u have faith and believe! I have learned that no matter what happens or how bad it seems today; life does go on and it will be better tomorrow.

Things to ponder on

Give and it will be given to you. Decide today to do something with your dreams. Disappoint procrastination and commit yourself to your potential. Stop wishing and start willing. Stop proposing and start purposing. See your dream. Speak your dream. Live your dream.

APRIL 20

Blessed are those who understand God's in control. Leave certain things in His hands and you will be fine.

Things to ponder on

Dear Past, I can't go back the way things used to be. It's time to move on. I have a future that's waiting on me.

APRIL 21

Faith will get you to and through any situation you encounter. Pray and let God be God.

Things to ponder on

There comes a time when you have to choose between turning the page or closing the whole book!

APRIL 22

God intended for you to win, so let's continue to do so until He decides otherwise. It's amazing how God works when you stay positive and in faith.

Things to ponder on

If you keep telling people about your same problems, you don't want help, you want attention.

APRIL 23

For some reasons, God keeps on opening doors I didn't even knock on.

Things to ponder on

Keep your head to the sky. You are going to make it. You have to believe it.

APRIL 24

If you fall, you can get up again. If you lost your focus, you can be restored. If you still struggle, there is strength. God is your refuge and hope.

Things to ponder on

Some people don't need your judgment, they just need your prayers!

April 25

What God has for YOU is for YOU! There's no competition or negotiation!

Things to ponder on

One mistake I feel a person can make is to surround themselves with people whom they feel they have to impress.

APRIL 26

Life writes the script, but there's always room for a miracle when you cast God in the production.

Things to ponder on

Will we ever get away from texting and start having real conversations?

APRIL 27

God, I thank you for this day that wasn't promised to me. Be blessed and enjoy the beauty in your day.

Things to ponder on

If you believe in yourself, anything is possible.

APRIL 28

Help empower, inspire, love someone today without any expectations! Sometimes you may feel like why isn't he hearing my cry, giving me what I want, or answering my prayer? But God knows our heart and He knows what we need. Trust Him completely. He has everything worked out for us. It's all in His plan. So be patient and keep praying, praising and thanking Him before its done. YOUR TIME IS NEAR so NAME IT, CLAIM IT and RECEIVE IT!

Things to ponder on

Discover your passion! Follow your heart! Create peace! Embrace change!

APRIL 29

Crutches are meant to be a temporary help; not meant for a lifetime. People can be crutches. YOU can become too dependent on your crutches and they can limit your growth. Know when it's time to move on. Know when someone's time in your life is over. Know that when God closes a door, He has something greater planned for you. God will give you people who are not just "with" you; they are "for" you.

Things to ponder on

When is the last time worrying change a situation for the better? Yeah, I can't remember either!

APRIL 30

God is love!

Things to ponder on

Always be what you want to be and not what people
want to see.

MAY 1

Worship is a lifestyle, not just a Sunday morning event. Worship God with your lifestyle throughout the week.

Things to ponder on

Don't follow your head, for it has no heart; don't follow your heart, for it has no logic; follow your soul...... it has both!

MAY 2

From every wound there is a scar and every scar tell a story. A story that says I have survived. In God we trust.

Things to ponder on

Old wounds need to heal so just let them heal.

MAY 3

God wants full custody of us and not on Sunday's visitation. God will exceed your expectation if given a chance!

Things to ponder on

Life is about trusting your feelings and taking chances, losing and finding happiness, appreciating the memories, learning from the past, and realizing people change.

MAY 4

Outward beauty reveals what we look like. Inner beauty reveals who we are. Walking with God causes us to reflect His beauty. May your spirit be blaze with the fire of God's love!

Things to ponder on

Don't be afraid to believe that you can have what you want and deserve. Strive for excellence in every aspect of your life!

MAY 5

When God gets you out of a situation, don't give credit to anyone but Him. You know He was the only one who did it.

Things to ponder on

If you're dealing with a person that can't tell you what it is, you already know what it's not.

MAY 6

Are you wrinkled with burden? Go to God for a faith lift. Count your blessings and not your troubles.

Things to ponder on

You are currently outgrowing people who don't want to grow!

May 7

Prayer can cause doors to open, addictions to be broken, eyes to be open, joy to be restored and strongholds to be destroyed. Trust and believe.

Things to ponder on

Life will keep bringing you the same tests over and over again until you pass it.

MAY 8

God is like a computer. He ENTERS your life, SCANS your problems, EDITS your tensions, DOWNLOADS solutions, DELETES your worries, and SAVES you.

Things to ponder on

Do not let your attitude be your disability! Don't block your blessing with complaints!

May 9

Ask God to correct you, direct you and protect you. Pray He does the same for someone else.

Things to ponder on

Love can take you many places but hate can limit where you go.

MAY 10

Whenever there is a GAP in your life, remember God Always Provides.

Things to ponder on

I admire people who choose to smile after all the things they've been through.

MAY 11

Broken leg, go to the doctor. Broken car, find you a mechanic.... broken spirit, go to the LORD!! GOD will give you an UNLIMITED lifetime warranty that never expires so whenever you find yourself broken take yourself back to the manufacturer.

Things to ponder on

Embrace struggle... It is your greatest teacher!

MAY 12

Peace be still! Today let go of the stress in your life! Relax your mind and allow God's peace to wash over you.

Things to ponder on

Sometimes a person just needs someone who will just listen. No words. No advice. Just a listening ear.

May 13

Sometimes God allows people to walk out of your life in order for someone better to walk in.

Things to ponder on

You will never have closure if you keep the door open!

MAY 14

Despite whatever you are going through, there is always hope. Keep the faith.

Things to ponder on

Try to stay humble because I know this blessing can be taken away any minute!

MAY 15

God didn't bring you out to deep waters to drown, He brought you here because your enemies can't swim.

Things to ponder on

The fastest way to kill something special, is to keep comparing it to something else.

MAY 16

Be wise enough to thank God for not giving you what you asked for and gracious enough to enjoy what He gave you instead.

Things to ponder on

Note to self: What you think is a setback may be a blessing in disguise!

MAY 17

Don't count your troubles. Instead count yourself being blessed every day and you will find yourself living in a world of blessings.

Things to ponder on

Most people are just talking and eating but never bring a dish to the table!

MAY 18

Whatever you feel is going wrong in your life, just say to yourself, "This too shall pass" and keep moving forward.

Things to ponder on

Being free is being comfortable in your own skin. No one can take your joy if you don't want them to have it.

MAY 19

I don't want to miss a single blessing that God has for me simply because I chose not to walk through the door that HE opened for me

Things to ponder on

Leave yesterday alone (it's gone). Live for today (count your blessings). Don't worry about tomorrow (it may not come).

MAY 20

I may be BENT, but not BROKEN, everything
happens for a REASON. Because if GOD brings you
to it, HE will bring you through it.

Things to ponder on

Love is a gift that some people may try, but you
can't buy it or find it. Someone has to give it to you.
Learn to be receptive of that gift.

MAY 21

Never ask God to order your steps if you are not ready to move your feet.

Things to ponder on

Life is worth the struggle when you can look back and realize you have more now than ever before.

MAY 22

God finds great usage for broken pieces. He is our potter. We are His clay. Let go of resentment, it will hold you back. Do not worry about what could have been. What is to come is what matters.

Things to ponder on

There's no traffic when you're in your own lane.

MAY 23

If you move to a new place with your old mind, you'll just do the same stuff, in a different place. Renew your mind. Allow God to shape and mold you in His own way.

Things to ponder on

Hurt people hurt people, because at some point they were hurt. Forgive yourself and them.

MAY 24

Today! Release disappointments before they make a home in your heart. Know from whom your blessings flow!

Things to ponder on

Never underestimate the power of a person's intuition. Some people can recognize game before you even play it!

MAY 25

Don't live in the past by holding on to "what was."
Live for what is and what will be! Trust that God has a
plan for you TODAY! Let the GOOD in your life speak
louder than the misfortune.

Things to ponder on

One of the hardest things is to open is a closed mind!
How many of us has to deal with someone like that
on a daily basis?

MAY 26

It's so hard living this life! If it's not one thing, it's another! Therefore, we have to keep pushing on the best way we know how!

Things to ponder on

People may give their opinions; however, their opinions don't have to dictate your life.

MAY 27

Be happy when God answers your prayers, but be more thankful when God makes you the answer to someone else's prayer!

Things to ponder on

If you lose someone because they have different intentions than you, you haven't "lost" anything. You've gained clarity.

May 28

In the bible James 1:13-15 states that those faced with temptations cannot blame God for their situation. We live by the decisions we make, so be wise in anything you decide.

Things to ponder on

Relationships are like sharing a book, it doesn't work if you're not on the same page.

MAY 29

There can be no victories without battles. There can be no peaks without valleys. No roses without thorns. With God's strength behind you, His love within you and His arms underneath you, you are more than sufficient for the days ahead of you.

Things to ponder on

Silence has a deep explanation in every situation. Somethings are just not worth a response.

MAY 30

Remember, people who fall the hardest bounce back the highest when God is involved. Your time is now. No one can stop you when God is blessing you. All they can do is get out the way.

Things to ponder on

STOP giving people the satisfaction of knowing they can get to you. Once you show them the button, they won't stop pushing it.

MAY 31

I have grown to appreciate the beauty of each day, which supersedes the negative attractions that pull us under and away from our true essence. We are laced within with a spirit that wants to love and laugh, and live an existence that embraces light and joy. I chose to embrace love, wrapped in the essence of light. Stay in the light and reach for the joy which exist within each one of you.

Things to ponder on

Expect nothing but anticipate everything. Just accepting each moment and appreciating the blessing in every lessons.

June 1

Despite the dark clouds and a little rain, the sun is still shining on you. Keep God's commandments. What's for you, will be for you.

Things to ponder on

The best things in life are free. A smile, hug, kind word, listening ear, or a soft touch. It won't cost you a thing to spread them all day to others. Be a blessing to someone today!

JUNE 2

You are a living testimony. Speak life.

Things to ponder on

When it's real, you will know. You won't be confused about it.

June 3

When you forgive, you heal. When you let go, you grow.

Things to ponder on

Appreciate what you have before its turn into what you had.

JUNE 4

If your problems have brought you to prayer, then they have served a purpose! Don't let ups and downs leave you down and out! Keep the faith!

Things to ponder on

The only people who should be a part of your circle are those who make the sun shine, not the ones who rain on your parade.

JUNE 5

Anywhere you travel, you will likely come to a point where two roads intersect and you must choose whether to turn or go straight. We all face intersections in our lives. They are our turning points, the place where we must make decisions. If you are standing at a point of decision in your life, follow wisdom and seek God with all of your heart.

Things to ponder on

Time to unwind! Lose the luggage. Whatever is weighing you down, put it down. Toss it to the side and travel light!

JUNE 6

Make PEACE with your broken PIECES.

Things to ponder on

You cannot give a person blessings that they are not ready for, even if that blessing is you.

June 7

Sometimes God closes doors because it's time for you to move FORWARD.

Things to ponder on

Be strong- A phrase that's easy to say but a hard thing to do when you are broken. Keep the faith!

June 8

Love, read and follow Gods words. Apply it to your life. You are never too young, but someday you may be too old.

Things to ponder on

I have a lot of love and respect for people who stay strong even when they have every right to break down. New day, new mindset. Let's have a positive day today.

June 9

People will test your faith on a daily basis! Just say to yourself in God's love I am blessed, chosen, adopted, favored, redeemed and forgiven! Just know you are protected by a shield of faith and the sword of the spirit which is God's word. Enjoy your day!

Things to ponder on

For many of us, life is not the way we imagined. It's just the way it is. The way you cope with it is what makes the difference. Continue to count your blessing and not your troubles.

June 10

Don't be afraid to make a change in your life if needed. Growth is change and to change in your life, you must change in your mind. We can't grow unless we submit to change and to God, who can righteously guide our change.

Things to ponder on

Nobody can get your spot because it has been ordained just for you!

JUNE 11

Live in truth. Walk in truth. Walk by Faith and not by sight.

Things to ponder on

Everyday spent above the ground is a day to be thankful for.

JUNE 12

Be encouraged. What you're going through, God will still get the glory. There is victory in your silence.

Things to ponder on

If you want to maintain a person's respect, DO what you say you are going to DO. These days, most people can write a book on broken promises.

June 13

Public Service Announcement: God is not through BLESSING you! Just hold on!

Things to ponder on

If you don't go after what you want, you will never have it. If you don't ask, the answer is always be no. If you don't step forward, you will always be in the same place.

June 14

Why are you still hanging on when God has confirmed for you to let go? Let it GO!

Things to ponder on

Your growth scares people who don't want to change.

June 15

When we arrive at a dilemma in our life and are
unable to decipher the right direction to go. If we
hope to maintain our joy in the process. We must
allow God to be our Guide, our Strength, our Wisdom
our all. We have to learn to trust God when we do not
understand what is happening in our lives.

Things to ponder on

Being in love is a responsibility because you have
someone else's heart in your hand.

June 16

To see without opening your eyes is vision. To take a trip without walking is a journey. To trust without question is Faith. When the hand of God is upon you, favor will come. Embrace it and receive it!

Things to ponder on

Even if it makes you mad. You have to respect the truth.

June 17

The bible says I can do all things through Christ which strengthen me. If we live in the spirit, let us also walk in the spirit.

Things to ponder on

If we could forget our troubles as easily as we forget our blessings, how different things would be. Feed your faith and your doubts will starve to death.

June 18

Dear God, today deposit faith in my account, withdraw stress, transfer understanding, balance my life and add interest.

Things to ponder on

Life is so much better with you in it! Enjoy the beauty in your day!

June 19

How do you spell life? T-R-U-S-T! In the midst of praise, prayer and surrender, you will learn to trust God.

Things to ponder on

Truth is the blanket that keeps you safe upon the bed of all other experiences.

June 20

Before you start your day today say a little prayer asking God to give the strength you need to accept people as they are and to help us all be more understanding of those who are different from us!

Things to ponder on

Be careful what you ask for, you might get it. Your words, your dreams, and your thoughts have power to create conditions in your life.

June 21

Don't let circumstances or situations steal your joy. Be determine to stay strong by being joyful. Let God's joy be complete in you. Knowing who we are in faith in God, gives us the confidence to move past mistakes we have made in the past and embrace the future with joy.

Things to ponder on

There are many who will come to draw from the well, once it has been filled. They were nowhere to be found when you were working hard and struggling to pour into it!

JUNE 22

Dear Lord, today take away what I don't need, add what I do, subtract any excess, divide distractions and multiply miracles.

Things to ponder on

A lot of people can't see who you are because they are too busy judging you for who you were. Let the past be the past.

JUNE 23

YOU are God's child. Whoever counted you out. Can't count.

Things to ponder on

Love shouldn't require Windex to be clear. It either is or it isn't!

JUNE 24

Do You have hope? If you believe in God and have hope, you probably have been blessed in many ways. The bible says I wait for the Lord, my souls waits, and in His words, I put my hope. Nothing ahead of you is going to be bigger or stronger than the power of God behind you.

Things to ponder on

Step out and use your gifts! The more you use your God-given potential, the more fulfilled and happier you will be. Let your light shine so the world can see!

June 25

Remember today is a new day and new possibilities! God will give you what you exactly need when you need it! Trust God and He will lead you in the right direction!

Things to ponder on

Remember that you're only as valuable as you make and present yourself to be! Know your worth, demand it, and have some self-respect.

JUNE 26

To everything there is a season. A time for every purpose under heaven. Whatever season we are in, it's always the season to trust in Him.

Things to ponder on

You are only as real as the amount of truth you keep in your life. Lying to yourself leads to lying to others.

JUNE 27

We often have to thank God for unanswered prayers.
Just giving us what we need instead of what we want.

Things to ponder on

Don't let ANYONE steal your joy - the world didn't
give it and the world can't take it away!

June 28

I have learned: To put God first in all I do. Peace of mind is the greatest fortune. Long sustaining health is the greatest possession. Joy is the best emotion. Loving and being loved is the greatest feeling!

Things to ponder on

Never apologize for how big or blessed your life is. Only those who don't belong in it will ask you to.

JUNE 29

Can God use you in this season? Yes, He can but you must be spiritually and emotionally available.

Things to ponder on

Sometimes we have to go through the worst just to become our best. Let the struggle shape you and not break you.

JUNE 30

God can bring you through situations you think you won't survive. He can make you comfortable in the most uncomfortable places, and give you peace in the midst of trauma. Before your life is over, you'll live, love, and experience loss. Losing some things will actually help you to appreciate the things you still have. You will live each day not knowing what tomorrow holds. No, all your tomorrows are in God's hands.

Things to ponder on

We never fully understand what people go through until we go through it ourselves.

July 1

God will never put you in a position to do something without giving you the strength and the ability to do it.

Things to ponder on

The eyes are the mirror to the soul. Seek your purpose and everything else will flow. No matter what walk of life you're from, you can be sure of four things. That hope will get you through the worst of times and love will always mend your wounds.

July 2

Today is your day. Leave all the drama, the pain, the negativity, and the self-doubt behind. Blessings aren't always material things. One of the best blessings is simply blessing others.

Things to ponder on

What we do in life, echoes in eternity. Remember: never look down on someone unless you're trying to lift them up!

July 3

Sometimes, we spend so much time angry at the past that we forget to REJOICE over the lessons it taught us! IT happened. The good news is, IT'S OVER!

Things to ponder on

No one can string you along if you let go of the rope.

JULY 4

No matter what circumstances or trials you may face today, God is able to bring you through it.

Things to ponder on

If you don't believe in your own abilities, no one else will. You need to buy into your own story.

July 5

Your trials are just shaping you for your blessing. Get ready to be mentally, physically and spiritually fit. Get in shape and be ready for the blessings.

Things to ponder on

No matter how big or small the step is just keep moving forward.

July 6

Stop being anxious and worrying about things that may never happen. Faith means that you can have peace even when you don't have all the answers. When you are trusting in God you don't need a plan B or a plan C, because you're trusting God's plan "A" for your life.

Things to ponder on

It's a humbling moment when you realize that what you wanted was not in your best interest!

JULY 7

Faith is the bridge between where I am and the place where God is taking me.

Things to ponder on

Some people never get the picture until they are out of the frame.

JULY 8

We come this far by faith. Can't turn around now.
Keep pressing on.

Things to ponder on

There is power in words. Speak things into existence!
Say it loud with your heart.

July 9

They worked behind the scenes to destroy you. But GOD worked behind "their" scenes to develop you!

Things to ponder on

Drugs make the best people do the worst things.

JULY 10

Despite the dark clouds and a little rain, the sun is still shining on you. Keep God's commandments. What's for you, will be for you. We can't expect God to order our steps when we're out of place.

Things to ponder on

Ease your mind, put your trouble to the side and just enjoy the beauty in your life. Be free. Be safe.

JULY 11

God is love. Step out on faith and see where its lead you. Even with your flaws, you are still God's masterpiece.

Things to ponder on

Don't entertain unnecessary drama! Be bigger and better than that!

JULY 12

Dear God, it's a new day. Please protect, rebuild, restore, and repair us!

Things to ponder on

Why do we spend money we don't have on things we don't need to impress people we don't like"? Just a thought!

July 13

Let your light so shine before people that they may see your good works and glorify God in Heaven. Put God first no matter what situation you're in, good or bad.

Things to ponder on

Where the Lord is leading you, everyone is not going to be able to follow. You can't raise a person up who wants to be dead.

July 14

Be confident and stoic. God has you alive to live. If you believe in Him and made in His image, you have to believe in you. Speak it, seek it, believe it, and receive it.

Things to ponder on

My soul looks back and wonder how I got over.

July 15

God, you are my friend. I didn't know until I lost my way, went astray and about to lose my mind. I kept looking around and didn't realize you were there all the time. It was your grace and mercy that got me through.

Things to ponder on

Have you ever sat down and thought about how blessed you are?

JULY 16

In God, we trust! Trust in His timing. Rely on His promises. Wait for His answers. Believe in His miracles. Rejoice in His goodness. Relax in His presence.

Things to ponder on

All work. No play. Make a dull life. Don't forget to treat yourself. Why not? You deserve it.

July 17

Today, I was reminded about the power of God's love, it moves mountains, it heals wounds, it opens doors that have been closed.

Things to ponder on

You are only as real as the amount of truth you keep in your life. Lying to yourself leads to lying to others.

JULY 18

When you're hurting, the church can be like a spiritual hospital. It's a good place to visit and get healed.

Things to ponder on

The truth will always outrun and outlive a lie!

July 19

In the bible it states, "Be not afraid or dismayed at the great multitude for the battle is not yours, but God. Our minds plans our way, but God direct our steps.

Things to ponder on

We have all experienced disappointments and hurts, but we have to maintain an open heart. You have to be willing to be hurt if you truly want to love. You have to be willing to be disappointed if you really want to know how to trust. It's called life and in life there is some pain. There is also a whole lot of joy and happiness.

JULY 20

In life we go through stages but some of us ends up getting stuck in phases. Just continue to trust in the Lord with all your heart, and lean not on your own understanding. In all your ways acknowledge Him and He shall direct your paths.

Things to ponder on

Are you crippling someone that is able to walk on their own because you insist on carrying them, their responsibility, their mistakes, their life? We must learn to let go!

July 21

God is love. I don't say i love you just to hear you say it back. I say it so you want forget. Tomorrow is not promise. Enjoy your day.

Things to ponder on

You ever thought that perhaps the reason why you can't get what it is you want! Is because its isn't what God want you to have!

July 22

I have been through the storm and the rain. I made it. Had to overcome some heartache and pain. Yet I still made it. The devil tried to keep me down. God keeps on blessings me round and round. Now point to yourself and say I made it!

Things to ponder on

Dear past, stop tapping me on my shoulder! I have no plans on looking back. Only focusing on looking and going forward!

July 23

Sometimes the wrong choices bring us to the right places if we just allow ourselves to let go of the wheel at some point and let God steer us.

Things to ponder on

One of the toughest battles you have to fight is between what you know and what you feel.

JULY 24

My faith reminds me that there is 'value in the valley'. We go through tough times to learn to appreciate the good. Never forget the pain and struggle you've been through. Use that to fuel your present faith and lead you to your blessed future.

Things to ponder on

Shout out to all the parents out there who sacrifice to make sure their children have a chance at a better life. We continue to celebrate you.

July 25

Do not let your past hurts be your future pains. Too many times we let the past hold on to us because we still holding on to the past. It's a new day. let it go. Sorrow looks back. Faith moves forward.

Things to ponder on

Love can take you many places, but hate can limit where you go!

July 26

No one can stop you when God is blessing you. All they can do is get out the way.

Things to ponder on

Someone that is 100% down for you and got your back is something money can't buy.

JULY 27

God build a fence around us. Protect us. Guide us. Still part of Gods holy plan. Still holding on to your hand.

Things to ponder on

The heart only holds room for openness and love. Jealousy cannot exist in it!

JULY 28

Blessed is a person who understands the reason for praying isn't to have all he or she wants, but to thank God for all he's given!

Things to ponder on

Let the beauty of what you love be what you do.

July 29

We are like pencils. Our true worth lies within us. We are in God's hands and He uses us. We are sharpened in life by events and situations. We are also expected to leave a mark.

Things to ponder on

Repeat after me, "I am no longer a victim of my past or circumstances. I am a survivor! Nothing and nobody can stop me now! Too blessed to be stressed!

JULY 30

When you have come to a crossroad in your life. Things are not just going right. You have to say and believe that this too shall pass.

Things to ponder on

Stars can't shine without darkness. You are a diamond continue to shine like one today.

July 31

God always uses situations as an opportunity for us to see peoples' true colors. All we have to do is be open to hear, see and identify what's put before us. What we think is, is really not and what we believe is not, really is.

Things to ponder on

Protect your spirit. Not everyone deserves access to you.

AUGUST 1

God is love! Let's see with love! Think in love! Move in love! Live as love! Love is me! Love is you! Be love!

Things to ponder on

If it doesn't agree with your spirit then let it go! Appearance is nothing if you're empty on the inside!

August 2

We have to learn to trust God when we do not understand what is happening in our lives.

Things to ponder on

I learned a long time ago not to judge people by what they look like, sound like, or the clothes they wear. Just because a house is nice and shiny out front, doesn't mean that it's not rotting inside.

August 3

God may remove you from your comfort zone because you are not moving forward.

Things to ponder on

Many people are trying to move on without HEALING! I don't think that is possible. The most attractive quality you can carry into a new relationship is your OWN happiness!

AUGUST 4

In the bible it states," Only fear the Lord, and serve Him in truth with all your heart; for consider what great things he has done for you." We can't undo yesterday, but we can act today to influence tomorrow. Don't let yesterdays failures bankrupt tomorrow's efforts. Look ahead and seek God's way.

Things to ponder on

A lot of times we will block our own blessings by the decisions we make.

August 5

Hope + Faith = Patience. Anything worth having requires a lot of patience to receive. Gods walk with you even when you are alone!

Things to ponder on

Expect nothing but anticipate everything. Accepting each moment and appreciating the blessing in every lesson.

AUGUST 6

No mountain is bigger than your faith! God's delays are not God's denials. God has His own clock. God is never too late and never too early.

Things to ponder on

Choose people who choose you.

August 7

If it weren't for God being on your side, where would you be?

Things to ponder on

If you have people in your life that push you, pray for you, and encourage you, embrace that. It's because they see the best in you!

August 8

In the bible, Proverbs states, "That where there is no vision, people perish." A vision is something we see in our mind. It may be what God plants in us or something we see on purpose. It is the way we think about ourselves, past or future. It does not cost anything to believe. Don't have a "give up easy" attitude. Let your faith soar. Be creative with your thoughts. Believe you can do whatever you need to do in life through Christ.

Things to ponder on

Excuses- Ain't got time for that. Either you are going to do what you say or you are not.

AUGUST 9

Remember today is a new day with new possibilities. God will give you what you need exactly when you need it. Trust God and He will lead you in the right direction.

Things to ponder on

Step out and use your gifts. Let your light shine so the world can see.

August 10

God will sometimes put you in a place where you are out of your comfort zone to show you what He can do through you in spite of your struggle. Trust and believe.

Things to ponder on

You know you have grown when you have lost complete interest in not looking back. Letting it all go and moving forward.

AUGUST 11

Prayer does what money can't. Trust and believe that God is always good consistently, effortlessly and faithfully.

Things to ponder on

Everything isn't for everybody. Your heart, mind, soul, self-respect, dignity, pride, time, space, emotions, thoughts, future plans and most of all your LOVE! Be true to you!

August 12

It all can be gone by tomorrow. Always remember that and count your blessings. Not your troubles.

Things to ponder on

Gossip and hearsay can lead to a lot of misunderstanding. Know the facts before you speak on it.

August 13

Don't quit! Just pray it off of you. You will get through this because you're a survivor. Keep the faith.

Things to ponder on

Chin up or your crown will slip. Know you are God's best.

AUGUST 14

Don't always seek an instant return when you do God's will, but hold on to the promise because God is faithful.

Things to ponder on

Never tolerate disloyalty. Remember your soul is royalty.

AUGUST 15

God, I thank you for always being with me through my joys and pain. We at times have to learn to love the sunshine as well as the rain. If it didn't ever rain in our lives, we wouldn't know how to appreciate the sunshine.

Things to ponder on

Don't tell people your plans Just show them the results.

AUGUST 16

Your blessings will always outweigh the battle you are going through Keep the faith. Keep moving forward. Victory is yours.

Things to ponder on

People will try and kill the NEW YOU by telling everyone about the OLD YOU.

AUGUST 17

God will put you back together right in front of people who broke you.

Things to ponder on

You will never win someone's trust with promises. They have heard enough of those to realize they paint pictures that aren't accurate. Actions will always speak louder than words.

August 18

The bible says, "I can do all things through Christ which strengthen me" and "If we live in the spirit, let us also walk in the spirit."

Things to ponder on

Even if it makes you made, you have to respect the truth.

August 19

The things that are to happen in life are already written. The best thing you can do is pray and ask God for understanding.

Things to ponder on

Don't make a permanent decision on a temporary feeling. Never let your emotions guide you.

AUGUST 20

Live in truth and walk in truth. Walk by faith and not
by sight.

Things to ponder on

Everyday spent above the ground is a day to be
thankful for.

AUGUST 21

God is with you, even at your very weakest. Never lose faith in Him, because He will never lose faith in you.

Things to ponder on

Don't let negative and toxic people rent space in your head. Raise the rent and evict them. It's the weekend and we ain't got time for that.

August 22

Blessings don't have a schedule. We must be ready at all times. Are you ready?

Things to ponder on

You are a diamond. Make sure you shine brightly today!

August 23

If love and happiness can be found inside of you,
you'll never go a day without it. At the end of the day,
if God is all you have, you have all you need.

Things to ponder on

Be too grown to entertain drama and too wise to
entertain lies.

AUGUST 24

Today is the day the Lord has made! Stand on your hopes, your dreams. Don't allow anyone to disrupt your aspirations! When God opens a door, no man can close. When He closes a door, no man can open. Wait with patience and confidence, and your dreams will sprout into being (Rom. 8:24-25). Have a great day!

Things to ponder on

It can take years to get past your past but one conversation with the wrong person can to take you all the way back to the beginning. As a part of growth, you have to grow out of some people. A friend of your weakness is an enemy to your greatness. When you move on in life, learn to pack light, and only take the people and the thoughts that can grow with you. If they can't grow with you, they can't go with you.

AUGUST 25

These days we all need a little faith to get us through.
Faith gives the strength to go when we want to give
in. The courage to get up when we want to lie down.
Faith can't lift you up until life has knock you down.

Things to ponder on

Happiness will never come to those who fail to
appreciate what they already have.

AUGUST 26

Sometimes disappointments are just God's way of saying "I've got something better. Be patient, live life, have faith. "

Things to ponder on

LOYALTY still exists...We just got to stop being so loyal to the wrong people

August 27

The Blessed don't beef with the miserable. No one can take your joy if you don't want them to have it.

Things to ponder on

No person is your friend or mate who demands your silence or denies your right to grow.

AUGUST 28

Pray through it. Grow through it. Whatever you are going through, blessings cannot be chased. They must be claimed.

Things to ponder on

If people cannot see you shining, it is because their minds and eyes are cloudy!

August 29

When God doesn't have your attention, He may disturb what does.

Things to ponder on

Live your life like a tree. Stay connected to your roots, yes! But always keep growing, and continue to branch out in new directions.

AUGUST 30

Every door that has a handle is not meant for you to turn it. Trust that God will open the doors you need to enter and close the ones you don't!

Things to ponder on

Friendship is friendship. Business is business.

AUGUST 31

Live happy! Love everyone! Laugh often and learn
daily! Your thoughts can be your prison or they can
set you free to soar! You see my glory but you don't
know my Story.

Things to ponder on

I choose to be happy no matter what. It is good for
my soul. It's is good for my health.

September 1

Don't let prayer be your last resort in a time of need, make it your first. Praise comes naturally when u count your blessings.

Things to ponder on

No matter how much you revisit the past there's nothing new to see!

SEPTEMBER 2

Decide today to live with peace and not do more than you can handle! Count your blessing and not your troubles!

Things to ponder on

A true friend is someone who understands your past, believes in your future, and accepts you just the way you are."

SEPTEMBER 3

What are you seeking! What are you looking for! How do you know if God has already blessed you with it? The bible says i sought the lord, and he heard me and delivered me from all my fears. I will bless the lord at all times, his praise shall continually be in my mouth.

Things to ponder on

Stop looking for the magic. You are it.

SEPTEMBER 4

Prayer does what money can't. Trust and Believe that God is ALWAYS good consistently, effortlessly, faithfully.

Things to ponder on

Sometimes we create our own heartbreak through expectations.

SEPTEMBER 5

Today is a new day. In order to be at peace, YOU have to become okay with your testimony.

Things to ponder on

A lie may take care of the present but it has no future.

September 6

Do not despair, the help you need will come, when you lift your heart and mind in prayer towards the Heaven above! Count your blessing and not your troubles!

Things to ponder on

If you live long enough, life will humble u. Life will level your defenses, expose your bad habits, and reveal self-inflicted nonsense! Learn, love and live!

SEPTEMBER 7

God will sometimes put you in a place where you are out of your comfort zone to show you what He can do through you in spite of your struggle. Trust and believe.

Things to ponder on

You know you have grown when you have lost complete interest in not looking back. Letting it all go and moving forward.

September 8

A mountain appears smaller when you start taking a few steps everyday towards the top.

Things to ponder on

It's better to know and be disappointed, than to never know and always wonder.

September 9

Good morning! Be blessed because you are! Make it your business to pray early, work smart, seek divine direction in all things. Love and Light.

Things to ponder on

A smile is an inexpensive way to improve your appearance. So, continue to smile.

SEPTEMBER 10

Trust the things that God blocks in your life. It will make sense later.

Things to ponder on

You don't need anyone's permission to be who you are!

SEPTEMBER 11

Speak life into all things and people you encounter today. Your words or acts just may be the difference for someone who has lost or losing hope. You just never know.

Things to ponder on

It's AMAZING that we pay people more to entertain us than we pay teachers to educate us. Priorities are backwards.

September 12

Today what's ever troubling you or challenges you may face. Turn it over to God. The battle is the lord not yours. Keep the faith.

Things to ponder on

I hate to say it! If you want to really piss somebody off...let God start blessing you with a nice car, nice house, a promotion on your job, or he bless you with a husband or wife. Watch how some people begin to hate for no reason!

September 13

Place your desires before God, pray about them and trust God to give them to u if and when they are right for u. Just because u don't see any changes taking place doesn't mean they aren't happening. Keep standing, Keep believing, Keep hoping because your breakthrough is coming!

Things to ponder on

People without visions, hopes, dreams, ambition, or desire to WIN will go out of their WAY to kill yours!

September 14

The spiritual meaning of love is measured by what it can do. Love is meant to heal. Love is meant to renew. Love is meant to bring us closer to God. In God's love you are blessed, chosen, adopted, favored, redeemed and forgiven!

Things to ponder on

Befriend the lost! Hug the hurt! Kiss the broken! Love the lonely! God is love!

SEPTEMBER 15

Get your fire back. It's not over until God says it's over. Keep the faith.

Things to ponder on

When life throws you something that you ain't quite ready for just make the catch then figure out what to do with it Patiently.

September 16

Today's forecast: mostly cloudy with a 100% chance of God watching over and protecting you from any storm that may come your way.

Things to ponder on

Gossip and hearsay can lead to a lot of misunderstanding. Know the facts before you speak on it.

September 17

Learning to let go of the wheel and let God lead. No matter what maybe going on around us. It's all good. "And we know that all things work together for good to them that love God, to them who are the called according to his purpose." Romans 8:28

Things to ponder on

We are sometimes quick to see the problems in our day and reluctant to focus on the joys in our lives. Regardless of your relationship status, think of the many people who love and the depth of their love for you. Feeling love and knowing that you are loved.

September 18

What is life worth if we are at war in our relationship with God, people and ourselves. Step into your destiny. If u don't like what u are getting out of life, take a look at what u are putting into life!

Things to ponder on

Some people are in your life for a REASON, then some are in your life for a SEASON, and then you have those that are for a LIFETIME. The hard part is trying to figure out who fits where.

September 19

We have to thank GOD for the "little" things he does for US like: Waking US up THIS morning, the activities of OUR limbs, a right mind... You know, the LITTLE things that we take for granted because a lot of us too busy waiting to be blessed by our OWN definition of the BIG things... You know, the Benz, or the Mansion on the hill. There is nothing wrong with that. I'd rather be grateful for the.... "LITTLE THINGS"

Things to ponder on

Chin up or your crown will slip. Know you are God's best.

September 20

The bible says When you pass through the waters, I will be with u; and the rivers, they shall not overflow u. Before your burden overcomes u, trust God to put his arms underneath you.

Things to ponder on

Love is meant to nourish you, not deplete, drain, or take all your oxygen.

September 21

If you're wondering if God still has a purpose for your life. If you're still living. HE DOES! Count your blessing and not your troubles!

Things to ponder on

YOU need no one's permission to be who you are!

September 22

Walk by Faith even when you can't see your way.

Things to ponder on

Most people are like commercials: sound good but
you know its false advertisement.

September 23

God, I thank you for always being with me through my joys and pains. We at times have to learn to love the sunshine as well as the rain. If it never rained in our lives, we wouldn't know how to appreciate the sunshine.

Things to ponder on

I am all for freedom of expression! But don't let it block your blessing.

September 24

Understand, God has you exactly where He wants you. If you'll learn to be happy where you are, God will take you where you want to be!

Things to ponder on

Don't feel guilty doing what's best for you.

SEPTEMBER 25

We may go around complaining about our problems and spending half our time trying to figure out what we can do to solve them. We do everything except ask God, that we may receive that our joy may be full. In order for Him to give us what we need, we must be humble enough to quit trying and start trusting. We must be willing to stop doing and start asking.

Things to ponder on

If God is the DJ, then Life is the dance floor. Love is the rhythm and You are the music!

September 26

If you let your praise overpower your problems, your worship will silence your worry.

Things to ponder on

Please stop complaining about someone not treating you right, because if you deserve better, why are you still with them?

September 27

Repeat after me: I am no longer a victim of my past or circumstances. I am a survivor! Nothing nor nobody can stop me now. Too blessed to be stressed!

Things to ponder on

Be conscious of the type of people you attract and let in your life because sometimes they are there because you've allowed them to be!

September 28

My faith reminds me that there is 'value in the valley'. We go through tough times to learn to appreciate the good

Things to ponder on

It's not about who you've been with, it's about who u end up with. Sometimes the heart doesn't know what it wants until it finds what it wants!

September 29

Blessed is a person who understands the reason for praying isn't to have all he or she wants, but to thank God for all he's given!

Things to ponder on

The only people who should be a part of your circle are those who make the sun shine, not the ones who r Not everyone is meant to stay in your life. Many will be a lesson. Learn from it and move on.

September 30

God didn't promise days without pain, laughter without sorrow or sun without rain. But God did promise strength for the day, comfort for the tears and a light for the way. For all who believe in him. He answers their faith with everlasting love.

Things to ponder on

If your relationship status says "complicated" than u might as well be single! There is no in-between love! It either is or it isn't Just saying!

OCTOBER 1

God, no matter how high I get, I still will be looking up to You.

Things to ponder on

You can't build with someone who expect you to do all of the work.

OCTOBER 2

Believe everything happens for a reason. If GOD gives YOU a second chance, grab it with both hands. If it changes your life, let it.

Things to ponder on

Step out of your comfort zone and enjoy your day! Let go of the old and prepare yourself to embrace the new! Live your life!

OCTOBER 3

You ever thought that perhaps the reason you can't get what it is you want! Is because its isn't what God want you to have!

Things to ponder on

No regrets! I am just been blessed to see another day! Still finding my way. YOU have to continue to go forward despite the mistakes you made along the way. Sending love in all directions on this day!

October 4

For it is a new day let yesterday's troubles be yesterday's troubles awake afresh and anew, smile put yourself in a happy place and remember for He deemed you fit to awake so take this chance to correct your past mistakes by MOVING FORWARD and living with NO REGRETS

Things to ponder on

Whatever the situation may be, sometimes you have to know when to step back. Then move on.

OCTOBER 5

Release fear. Embrace Faith. Claim what is already yours while unloading unnecessary baggage. Make room for your blessings. It's okay. What God has for you will be for you.

Things to ponder on

Mothers and Fathers, you are the gardeners to the hearts of your children. They would not blossom without you.

October 6

I know in this journey called life. I don't want to walk alone. God be with me. Without you i can't make it on my own.

Things to ponder on

A Good Friend! How many of us can say we have them? One of the challenges in life is to find someone who knows all your flaws, differences and mistakes and yet still sees the best in you. One love!

OCTOBER 7

God's grace can give anyone a fresh start. Your past and history doesn't change the love God has for you. You are too strong to break. No weapon formed against you will prosper.

Things to ponder on

The truth may hurt but better a hurt from a truth than to be confronted by lies.

OCTOBER 8

Put all of your trust and expectation in God and not in people.

Things to ponder on

The only people who should be a part of your circle are those who make the sun shine, not the ones who rain on your parade.

OCTOBER 9

The enemy has no jurisdiction over your blessings! GPS won't work because he can't go near God's Positioning Strategies.

Things to ponder on

Sometimes you got to create your lane. And know how to stay in your lane!

OCTOBER 10

God won't give you a cross you cannot carry. He knows how much you can bear.

Things to ponder on

When you are not exactly where you want to be, remind yourself that neither are you where you used to be.

OCTOBER 11

Sometimes God closes doors because it's time for you to move FORWARD.

Things to ponder on

Big shout out to everyone who are living out their dreams and enjoying what you do!

October 12

Don't miss out on a gift from God just because it is not packaged the way you expect it! Cast your cares on God; that anchor holds!

Things to ponder on

I have a lot of love and respect for people who stay strong even when they have every right to break down. New day, new mindset. Let's have a positive day today.

OCTOBER 13

God will help you be all you can be, but He will never help you to be someone else.

Things to ponder on

If someone really wants to be with you, they'll be shouting it from the rooftop and not sweeping you under the rug!

OCTOBER 14

Despite the dark clouds and a little rain. The sun is still shining on you. Keep God's commandments. What's for you, will be for you.

Things to ponder on

You would not be who you are today if you had not been through what you went through. It didn't break you it saved you.

OCTOBER 15

What God has for YOU is for YOU! There's no competition or negotiation!

Things to ponder on

Don't let negative and toxic people rent space in your head. Raise the rent and evict them.

OCTOBER 16

No matter how long we have walked with god. We still have days that seem dark. In those times we still have to rely on who He is.

Things to ponder on

People come into your life and people leave it. You just have to trust that life has a road mapped out for you. In which the roads of life have its twists and turns and no two directions are ever the same. Yet our lessons will come from the journey, not the destination.

October 17

Me, personally I don't thank God enough. I may not be rich with money, but I am rich in other areas of my life. Thank you, God.

Things to ponder on

Sometimes you got to mess up to wake up.

October 18

Faith will get you to and through any situation you encounter. Pray and let God be God!

Things to ponder on

I don't dislike anybody. I just don't deal with everybody.

OCTOBER 19

Today is the day the Lord has made, treasured and planned. We'll not only be glad but we'll forget our worries and pain and focus on this day that God has made for us. Count your blessing and not your troubles

Things to ponder on

If you continue to be with the person that is not meant for you, you won't have room for the one who is.

OCTOBER 20

My good days outweigh my bad days, so I won't complain. God is love.

Things to ponder on

The sooner you let GO of the things/people that are pulling you down, the sooner you'll be visually CLEAR to SEE what's BEST for you!

OCTOBER 21

Our needs will never exhaust Gods supply!

Things to ponder on

Don't repeat chapters, the story will never change!

OCTOBER 22

We must learn to pick our battles. There are simply too many conflicts in life to fight them all. We will have many major things to deal with so the least we can do is try to let go all of the little things that people do to irritate us. People will try to tested your faith daily. The bible says Don't be amazed at the fiery trails that u go through because they are taking place to test your quality.

Things to ponder on

Cheating is pointless when being single is always available.

OCTOBER 23

Stop thinking someone owes you something, get to it and do it yourself. Rely on GOD, he is your "ONLY" source. See it and be it, speak it into existence. You are holding u back, stop blaming others. This Is Your Time. What Are You Waiting For?

Things to ponder on

Sometimes when you think the grass is greener on the other side you step over and find a lot of dirt. No grass no flowers just dirt.

OCTOBER 24

I thank God for His blessings every day. It could have been you or me that didn't wake up this morning.

Things to ponder on

A candle loses nothing by lighting another candle. Each one teach one!

OCTOBER 25

Breaking news! Despite your problems, flaws, shortcomings. God is still Accessible. God is still Reachable. Just seek him.

Things to ponder on

There is a big difference between who we love, who we settle for and who we are not meant for!

OCTOBER 26

No one can stop you when God is blessing you. All they can do is get out of the way.

Things to ponder on

Be thankful for the difficult times. During those times you grow. Be thankful for your mistakes. They will teach you valuable lessons.

OCTOBER 27

The bible says " Therefore humble yourselves under the mighty hand of God, that He may exalt you in due time, casting all your care upon Him, for He cares for you ".1 Peter 5:6-7. Be thankful for your troubles that's when they become your blessing.

Things to ponder on

Do not let your past hurts be your future pains. Too many times we let the past hold on to us because we still holding on to the past. It's a new day. let it go. Sorrow looks back. Faith moves forward.

OCTOBER 28

We all have been through something. We all have a story to tell. Your greatest life messages and your most effective testimony will come out your deepest hurts. That means that other people are going to find healing in your wounds and your words. God blessed us to be a blessing to someone. Continue to be that blessing.

Things to ponder on

It is better to be alone, Than in the wrong company. Tell me who your best friends are, and I will tell you who you are. If you run with wolves, you will learn how to howl. If you associate with eagles, you will learn how to soar to great heights.

October 29

Prayers and love are some of the best gifts anyone can receive. They're FREE, no cost, yet plenty of reward.

Things to ponder on

It's going to be a good day. A day to talk a walk, be free, reach out to someone you haven't talk to in a while, spread love, treat yourself. Peace and blessing to all.

OCTOBER 30

Every door that has a handle is not meant for you to turn it. Trust that God will open the doors you need to enter and close the ones you don't!

Things to ponder on

Presentation is everything. Represent well.

October 31

We will never really have it all together. Its ok to step outside the box. Too many times we limit ourselves. God is still God all day every day. No one can spoil your day without your permission. Most people will be about as happy, as they can be.

Things to ponder on

Be thankful for the trials, lessons, and the blessings! What don't hurt you will only make you stronger!

November 1

The bible states that we need to learn how to live from faith to faith. Which means we need to approach everything we face, every challenge we meet, every decision we make and everything we do with faith. Faith should be the posture of our hearts and the attitude of our minds toward every situation. Living by faith is not a feeling we have. Just a conscious decision we make

Things to ponder on

No price is too high when paying for a piece of mind.

November 2

Whatever your trial. God sees. Whatever your struggle. God knows. Whatever your needs, God will provide. Trust and believe

Things to ponder on

Growing old is mandatory. Growing UP is optional. People will only do, what you keep allowing them to do.

NOVEMBER 3

TRUST is the word for the day! We have to learn to trust God when we do not understand what is happening in our lives.

Things to ponder on

Confidence is the ability to feel beautiful without anyone telling you. When you feel good. You look good.

NOVEMBER 4

Your setback was a setup for your comeback! Count your blessing and not your troubles!

Things to ponder on

Rich or poor is a mindset. Spend your time giving!
Do it for the cause and not the applause!

November 5

No one said that life and this road i must travel would be easy. God i know u didn't bring me this far to leave me. Weave in the faith and God will find the thread.

Things to ponder on

Being in a relationship can be somewhat like sharing a book. It doesn't work if you're not on the same page.

NOVEMBER 6

In life we go through stages but some of us ends up getting stuck in phases. Just continue to trust in the Lord with all your heart, and lean not on your own understanding. In all your ways acknowledge Him and He shall direct your path.

Things to ponder on

You can't force the wrong person to be right for you.

NOVEMBER 7

God can turn obstacles into opportunities! Keep on moving!

Things to ponder on

Be at Peace with your past! Let go of whatever you feel may be holding you back. Keep moving forward.

NOVEMBER 8

The bible talks about how do you benefit if you gain the whole world but lose or forfeit your soul in the process.

Things to ponder on

Love comes to those who still hope even though they've been disappointed, believe even though they've been betrayed and to those who still love even though they've been hurt before.

NOVEMBER 9

As the song says, "We all fall down but we must get back up!" So, continue to love after losing and smile through those tears. Trying again once you've failed, accepting the lesson when you think you know it all. Rising in the face of certain adversity takes the kind of strength possessed by winners! God won't give you more than you can bear. Know that God is watching over you.

Things to ponder on

The tongue weighs almost nothing, but only a few people can hold it.

NOVEMBER 10

You can't break a person who seeks their happiness from God.

Things to ponder on

You can't show love if you don't know love.

NOVEMBER 11

Be too blessed to be stressed. Speak life into your soul.

Things to ponder on

In life, you're going to be left out, talked about, lied to and maybe used, but you have to decide who's worth your tears and who's not!

November 12

If we could forget our troubles as easily as we forget
our blessings. How different things would be. Feed
your faith and your doubts will starve to death.

Things to ponder on

Trust before you love. Know before you judge.
Commit before you promise. Forgive before you
forget. Appreciate before you regret.

NOVEMBER 13

Looking forward to another great day. Remember the battle is not yours. It's God.

Things to ponder on

Life is what you make it. Choose joy, peace, love and happiness!

NOVEMBER 14

Live today free from sorrow, bother, anger, jealousy and malice. Engrave onto your heart one phrase: Today is my only day. Yesterday has passed with its good and evil and tomorrow has not yet arrived. Live for today. Pray with a thankful heart and remember the almighty with sincerity.

Things to ponder on

Love is always full time. Never part time. Never sometimes and certainly not just on your time.

NOVEMBER 15

Sometimes when you are working on changing your own life, you want to take your friends on the journey with you. God determines who walks into your life. It is up to you to decide who you let walk away, let stay, and refuse to let go!

Things to ponder on

A relationship that's is draining everything you put into it, has a crack in its foundation.

November 16

I know that God knows best! It's really hard to let someone go when you don't want to let go. Especially, when sickness overtook their body and fear of the end is near. No one knows the day nor the hour but God!

Things to ponder on

You have to endure the storm to see the rainbow. Everyone wants happiness, no one wants pain, but you can't make a rainbow without a little rain.

November 17

May your soul rests in God alone. Gods plan for your life far exceeds the circumstances of your day!

Things to ponder on

When you put a person in certain place in your life, make sure they want be there and if they can handle the position.

November 18

Life does not center around you and I, but rather on God. He is the source and sustainer of life. It is by His will that we were created. It is by His will that we are given opportunity to choose to love or not love Him. It is by God's grace that we can see, hear, touch and experience life to the fullest.

Things to ponder on

We may go around complaining about our problems and spending half our time trying to figure out what we can do to solve them. Faith is not asking when, how and why. It's your journey but not always your directions. Enjoy the ride!

NOVEMBER 19

God will hide your future from those who are not supposed to join you in your promised land. They will think that nothing good will ever come from you. What God is really doing is clearing them out of the way to make room for greater blessings that they were never assigned to share with you.

Things to ponder on

People can be like milk. They have an expiration date. Just don't know when they may go bad on you.

NOVEMBER 20

When in doubt and your spirit is low, just say, "God help me to believe what I can be and all that I am. Show me the stairways I have to climb. For my sake just teach me one day at a time." Even if you can't see it, Gods light is always shining on you.

Things to ponder on

Sometimes you have to fall back to get a better view.

NOVEMBER 21

Worship is a lifestyle, not just a Sunday morning event. Worship God with your lifestyle throughout the week.

Things to ponder on

You can't always help who you fall for. No matter how hard you try and you just want to be with them or just talk to them. You never stop trying to make them happy by the little things you say or do because that's what makes you happy. Keep on living!

November 22

Broken leg, go to the doctor. Broken car, find you a mechanic. Broken spirit, go to the Lord! God will give you an unlimited lifetime warranty that will never expire so whenever you find yourself broken, take yourself back to the manufacturer.

Things to ponder on

Many times, we are fed lie after lie that it becomes truth to us. We can't remain tied to the lies. Life is a book and it has many different chapters!

NOVEMBER 23

Dear God, speak over me, my life, family and friends. If we ever need you, we need you right now. Build a fence around us and protect us from anything that is trying to harm us.

Things to ponder on

When a woman loves a man, she only loves that man. The only person who can mess that up is that man.

November 24

Seems like just the moment you get back on your feet, life sends you another storm to knock you back down. God will speak life into your storm. All you have to do is be still and weathered it. There is a brighter day ahead!

Things to ponder on

No one is immune to hard times! You too can someday be out of shape, broke, broken-hearted, or broken-spirited!

November 25

Never forget the pain and struggle you've been through. Use that to fuel your present faith and lead you to your blessed future.

Things to ponder on

When the love is real, it doesn't lie, cheat, pretend, hurt you, or make you feel unwanted.

November 26

The light of God enlightens every heart that draws close to Him. Where there is chaos, He can bring order. Where there is emptiness, He can bring fullness. Where there is darkness, He can bring light. No matter how deep the darkness is, it cannot overpower the light!

Things to ponder on

Understand that when you're trying to get yourself on track and live right, it's going to require separating yourself from those who aren't.

NOVEMBER 27

Psalm 28:7 states, "The Lord is my strength and my shield; my heart trusted in him, and I am helped: therefore, my heart greatly rejoiceth; and with my song will I praise him."

Things to ponder on

Sometimes life will take us where we didn't plan to go. Things may happen that's out of our control. Be strong and don't go for anything or settle for less. Because it's still your season to be blessed. Count your blessing and not your troubles.

NOVEMBER 28

What God has for you will be for you. No one can take that away. Don't worry about your haters. God will take your haters and turn them into blessing.

Things to ponder on

Men protect your women! Don't make her fall if you don't plan to catch her! Respect God's blessing!

November 29

Having patience with others is love. Patience with self is hope. Patience with God is faith! So, continue to be patient!

Things to ponder on

Welcome to today! Another day! Another chance! Feel free to change! Love speaks silently!

NOVEMBER 30

Outward beauty reveals what we look like. Inner beauty reveals who we are. Walking with God causes us to reflect His beauty. May your spirit blaze with the fire of God's love!

Things to ponder on

True love isn't found. It's built

DECEMBER 1

The bible states that we need to learn how to live
from faith to faith. Which means we need to approach
everything we face, every challenge we meet, every
decision we make and everything we do with faith.
Faith should be the posture of our hearts and the
attitude of our minds toward every issue. Living by
faith is not a feeling we have. Just a conscious
decision we make.

Things to ponder on

Be real, be happy, be unique, be true, be honest, be
humble, be true to yourself. Be like a computer.
Refresh your mind. Delete all your problems, undo
all your mistakes, and save all the happy moments.

December 2

This the day that God has made. I am grateful for the lesson and the blessing that has been bestowed upon me. Is there anything you are grateful for?

Things to ponder on

Most people allow their feelings to lead them through each day. They make decisions about what to do, where to go and who to spend time with based on how they feel. Feelings are based on emotions. They can go up or down like a rollercoaster. Acknowledge your feelings, but realize they are only feelings and pray, seek God and allow him to be your guide.

DECEMBER 3

Prayer changes things. Pray over it. Pray through it.

Things to ponder on

At times we can be our own worst enemy. Doubting ourselves of our capabilities. God will open a door of opportunity for us. It's up to us to walk through that door.

December 4

I pray for peace in the minds of those that have worry on their hearts. I know it's hard to sleep, to rest peacefully when trouble fills your heart. I pray God gives you the strength to LET GO of your past, your worries, or anything that's causing you paint. Keep the faith.

Things to ponder on

For the people that are holding on by a thin thread. Please remember that Faith is unbreakable and it won't ever pop, no matter what. Pull yourself back UP!

December 5

If God removes you from your comfort zone, don't fight it. He not only sees where you are, He sees where you should be! Trust and Believe.

Things to ponder on

Whether its Big or small. A lie is still a lie.

DECEMBER 6

Instead of focusing on what you don't have, focus on all the blessings in front of you! Everyone can't go where God is taking you!

Things to ponder on

As you get older you realize not everything deserves a response, just a silent mental note.

December 7

At birth, God handed you a debit card called life!
Every decision you make is a swipe on that card.
How are you spending your life!

Things to ponder on

When fear knocks on your door send faith to answer.
Don't speak your fears speak faith. Whatever is in
your heart will come out your mouth. YOU will never
make any change of any kind without faith.

DECEMBER 8

The bible says" My soul, wait only upon God and silently submit to him; for my hope and expectation are from him."

Things to ponder on

Things we go through in life whether it's good or bad. Makes us who we are. Nothing has to happen for me to feel good! I feel good because I'm alive! Life is a gift, and I revel in it.

DECEMBER 9

God, if it be thy will, Today take the STAINS off me, pull STRENGTH out of me, put SOLID people around me and STRESS behind me!

Things to ponder on

A relationship should be built on God, Communication, Commitment, Trust, Honesty, Support, and Love.

DECEMBER 10

God has been good to me. Even on my worst days. I can still see His blessings.

Things to ponder on

Shout out to those who are living out their dreams and making them come true. I am on my way of doing the same thing.

DECEMBER 11

God is my help in my every need. My every hunger He feeds. God is my health; I can't be sick. My strength, unfailing quick. God walks beside me, guides my way. Through every moment of the day.

Things to ponder on

Not all gifts are free. Some may come with a price. So be careful before you decide to take the gift.

December 12

It's a new day! Leave all the drama, the pain, the negativity, and the self-doubt behind. Trust God. His track record is flawless.

Things to ponder on

Your talent is God's gift to you. What you do it with it is your gift back to God.

December 13

Honestly God makes paths your eyes never saw possible. Just walk into your season. Walk with faith!

Things to ponder on

Why do we spend money we don't have on things we don't need to impress people we don't like?

DECEMBER 14

Smile at your storm. It won't last always!

Things to ponder on

Once you stop looking for what you want. You will find what you need.

December 15

Everything happens for a reason. We have to learn to trust God when we do not understand what is happening our lives.

Things to ponder on

Did they lie to you about who they were or did you lie to yourself about who they were?

DECEMBER 16

The bible teaches us that our words have power, not just the power to communicate our thoughts and converse with one another, but the power to determine our future. The words we say expose our character, intelligence and predilections. The words we hurl into this world.

Things to ponder on

A person changes for two reasons. They either learned enough or suffered enough.

December 17

Fill my cup God and make me whole. More of You and less of me. Still holding on.

Things to ponder on

Closed mouths don't get fed and lazy hands don't count bread.

December 18

If you move to a new place with your old mind...you'll just do the same stuff, in a different place. Renew your mind. Allow God to shape and mold you in his own way.

Things to ponder on

If a person makes more withdrawals in your life than deposits, CLOSE THE ACCOUNT. IT'S LOSING INTEREST!

DECEMBER 19

God on the shelf, a soul can feel lost. God by my
side, I can feel my strength and help! With God on
your side, who can be against you?

Things to ponder on

Mistakes are a part of being human. Appreciate your
mistakes for what they are: precious life lessons that
can only be learned the hard way. Be thankful for
making it another day. You aren't promised
tomorrow, so make the best of every situation. If it is.

December 20

Stop thinking someone owes you something. Get to it and do it yourself. Rely on GOD, He is your "ONLY" source. See it and be it. Speak it into existence. You are holding you back. Stop blaming others. This Is Your Time. What Are You Waiting For?

Things to ponder on

Are you crippling someone that is able to walk on their own because you insist on carrying them? It is their responsibility, their mistakes, and their life. We must learn to let go!

DECEMBER 21

I don't know about you, but it's in my DNA to be blessed. You can fall to the ground and still rise above the clouds. Faith will get you through it all.

Things to ponder on

Envy is reserved for the lazy, uninspired and unwilling. What God has for you is for you.

DECEMBER 22

We spend our lives looking for a soulmate until we overlook the eternal soulmate. Love, read and follow God's word. Apply it to your life. YOU are never too young, but someday maybe too old. Count your blessing. Not your troubles.

Things to ponder on

To be balanced is what we all need in life. Mentally, physically, psychologically and spiritually. Balance will see you through the storms of life.

DECEMBER 23

Dear God, I know whatever comes my way, Your grace and strength is sufficient to carry me through.

Things to ponder on

Be a gift to others, which is to be opened in due time. Be a blessing to many that will be shared at the right time.

December 24

Your storm is not where God is going to leave you.
Your Storm is needed for God to lead you.

Things to ponder on

Drugs can make the best people do the worst things.

December 25

It amazing how some people pick and choose parts of the bible to justify things in their life they are doing. Don't use a verse or two. Try to READ, STUDY AND APPLY THE WHOLE BIBLE in your life!

Things to ponder on

It's a new day! Love where you are in your life, love who you are and love what you do.

DECEMBER 26

Thank God for your strength. Trust Him with your weakness.

Things to ponder on

In order to LISTEN you must first learn to be SILENT. Notice they are compiled by the exact same letters.

DECEMBER 27

God is my security guard. ANYTHING or ANYONE
who comes against me, has to go through God first.

Things to ponder on

Your faith will be the strongest thing you can wear
today! Wear it well!

DECEMBER 28

God is a God of chances. If you get another chance
in life, grab it with both hands. If it changes your life!
Let it.

Things to ponder on

YOU will never see the great things ahead of you, if
you keep looking at the bad things behind you!

DECEMBER 29

Who are you trying to please man, woman, child or God? If you please God, everyone else should be pleased. If not, pray for them.

Things to ponder on

Sometimes life will take you places you didn't plan to go. Life also come with an expiration date. So, live it to the fullest the best way you know how.

DECEMBER 30

Never look so long at what you have lost, that you cannot see what God has allowed you to find! Get lost in your spirituality, and find yourself! Be happy and count your blessings while others are adding up their troubles!

Things to ponder on

If you lose someone because they have different intentions than you, you haven't "lost" anything. You've gained clarity.

DECEMBER 31

To everything there is a season. A time for every
purpose under heaven. Whatever season we are in,
it's always the season to put your trust in God.

Things to ponder on

The minute you settle for less than you deserve, it is
when you get less than what you settled for. Don't be
afraid to believe that you can have what you want.
Strive for excellence in every aspect of your life!
Those who bring happiness to live.

ABOUT THE AUTHOR

Jason Jones is a native of Columbus, Ga. Now resides in Atlanta, Ga. The son of Mr. James (R.I.P) and Mrs. Johnnie Jones. Have 1 sister (Harriet) and one brother (Kenny). A 1995 graduate of Voorhees College. Begin writing at the age of 12. Now a freelance writer whose work has appeared in magazines local and national. Love to travel, good music and positive vibes. I am a fan of Inspiration. I like to inspire and be inspired. My favorite saying is, "I can do all things through Christ which strengths me."

All I can say is, "Don't be afraid to step outside of your comfort zone. You never know what you can achieved by doing so."

Acknowledgments

Aunt Wylene W, Aunt Betty S., Cousin Curtis and
Rev. Dr. Oberia B, Aunt Bertha K, Deloris W, Mary
and Monica C, Harriet and John J, Rhoda B, Gayle
G, Milton W, Nikita T, Kerry G,Tanya M, Walter D,
Anita B, Lori M, Lisa M,Jamie T, Stephanie W,
Juanita H Anna Lee V, Tim C, Donald J, Cliff M,
Aaron M, T. Byrd, Dawn and Trish C,Floyd G, Chris
L, Tony S, Hobart R, Mark M, Benton Family,
Robinson Family, Murphy Family, Crawford Family,
Jones Family, Boone Family, Pearson Family,
Gibson Family, Boodie Family,Blackburn Family,
Porter Family, Williams Family, Aunt Delphine
G(R.I.P.)
Thank you for encouraging me to write, Andrew P.
(R.I.P.) Thanks for the all the talks and advice.
Uncle Lincoln J. (R.I.P.), Paris P. (R.I.P.), Aunt
Louise B. (R.I.P.), Aunt Mildred B. (R.I.P.), Jackie P.
(R.I.P.), and Emma M. (R.I.P.). Truly missed!

Made in the USA
Columbia, SC
23 August 2021

43168270R00221